READING WITH JESUS™

PARENTS' BOOK

YOU CAN TEACH YOUR 4 OR 5 YEAR OLD CHILD TO READ IN 90 DAYS©

Rev. Dr. Carol McIlwain Edwards

AuthorHouse™
1663 Liberty Drive
Bloomington, IN 47403
www.authorhouse.com
Phone: 833-262-8899

Because of the dynamic nature of the Internet, any web addresses or links contained in this book may have changed
since publication and may no longer be valid. The views expressed in this work are solely those of the author and do not
necessarily reflect the views of the publisher, and the publisher hereby disclaims any responsibility for them.

Any people depicted in stock imagery provided by Getty Images are models,
and such images are being used for illustrative purposes only.
Certain stock imagery © Getty Images.

This book is printed on acid-free paper.

ISBN: 978-1-4389-3080-0 (sc)

Print information available on the last page.

Published by AuthorHouse 01/22/2022

authorHOUSE®

Table of Contents

DEDICATION

I dedicate this inspired work, READING WITH JESUS™ *You Can Teach Your 4 or 5 Year Old Child To Read In 90 Days* ©, to my Lord and Savior, Jesus Christ, who has expanded this vision and trailblazing ministry. It is helping parents teach their precious children to read "before" they enter school, thus laying a good spiritual and educational foundation. (Deuteronomy 6:4-9) As parents are teaching their precious little ones, parents are blessed by becoming closer to their children and more proficient in the skill of reading. This brings about more revelation of The Word Of God as they search and study. Jesus Is The Word Of God!

(John 1: 1-3 In the beginning was the Word, and the Word was with God, and the Word was God. 2. The same was in the beginning with God. 3. All things were made by Him; and without Him was not any thing made that was made.)

ABOUT THE AUTHOR

This inspired work, READING WITH JESUS™ *You Can Teach Your 4 or 5 Year Old Child To Read In 90 Days* ©, grew out of the experiences of the author, Rev. Dr. Carol McIlwain Edwards, with persons from pre-school age to college level and senior citizens. The problem of illiteracy stems from lack of knowledge of parents on how to teach their children to read (Hosea 4:6) and parental involvement. (Deuteronomy 6:4-9)

Rev. Dr. Carol McIlwain Edwards is a Holy Ghost Spirit-filled Christian who loves the Lord and is preparing parents to train up our precious children while teaching them to read with the Word of God. *Proverbs 22:6 Train up a child in the way he should go: and when he is old, he will not depart from it.*

We must teach and train our children "at all times". *Deuteronomy 6:4-9 states, 4. Hear, O Israel: The Lord our God is one Lord: 5. And thou shalt love the Lord thy God with all thine heart, and with all thy soul, and with all thy might. 6. And these words, which I command thee this day, shall be in thine heart: 7. And thou shalt teach them diligently unto thy children, and shalt talk of them when thou sittest in thine house, and when thou walkest by the way, and when thou liest down, and when thou risest up. 8. And thou shalt bind them for a sign upon thine hand, and they shall be as frontlets between thine eyes. 9. And thou shalt write them upon the posts of thy house, and on thy gates.*

The author has long since stopped complaining about the problem of illiteracy which brings about behavioral problems, etc., and has decided, after The Holy Spirit revealed to her that when children learn to read they should learn to read "With The Word Of God" so they will not be deceived by the many voices in the world. They will know the voice of Jesus Christ (John 10:1-5 and John 10:27) and how to apply His Word to their daily lives. This ministry is eliminating the problem of illiteracy "before" it begins with our pre-school aged children (**as early as 2 ½ years old**). In addition, **4** and **5** year old children are learning to read in **90 Days**. Thus, the author is wiping out the spirit of illiteracy from our generations across the United States and throughout the world, with the help of The Holy Spirit!

INTRODUCTION

This inspired work, READING WITH JESUS™ *You Can Teach Your 4 or 5 Year Old Child To Read In 90 Days©*, contains five instructional units. Each unit is divided into three sections (1) Reading Phonetic Words, (2) Reading Sight Words, and (3) Reading Sentences. In addition, there is a Supplementary Word List.

Parents, you can teach your **4 or 5 year-old children to read in 90 days**, completing the developmental version of READING WITH JESUS™ *You Can Teach Your 4 or 5 Year Old Child To Read In 90 Days©.* We want our children walking into the school equipped with reading skills and The Word Of God!

READING WITH JESUS™

You Can Teach Your 4 or 5 Year Old Child To Read In 90 Days ©

90-DAY SCHEDULE

Unit One	3 Sections	Completion Time By/And Or Before
	Reading Phonetic Words	15 days
	Reading Sight Words	
	Reading Sentences	
Unit Two	3 Sections	15 days
	Reading Phonetic Words	
	Reading Sight Words	
	Reading Sentences	
Unit Three	3 Sections	15 days
	Reading Phonetic Words	
	Reading Sight Words	
	Reading Sentences	
Unit Four	3 Sections	15 days
	Reading Phonetic Words	
	Reading Sight Words	
	Reading Sentences	

Unit Five	3 Sections	15 days
	Reading Phonetic Words	
	Reading Sight Words	
	Reading Sentences	

Instructions for the Supplementary Word list	15 days

- Your child(ren) may complete the units in less time!

Parents, we are the primary educators of our children and, for the most part, we lack the knowledge we need to prepare our children to succeed in school. The Lord states in Hosea 4:6 *My people are destroyed for lack of knowledge.* This is evident by the illiteracy problem that plagues our nation today. What better way to introduce our children to the skill of reading than to teach them to read with that special ingredient, "The Word Of God"!

The Lord commands in *Proverbs 22:6, Train up a child in the way he should go: and when he is old, he will not depart from it.* The Lord has entrusted us to rear children, but they belong to Him. They are not our possessions, but God's. (*Psalm 127:3* states, *Lo, children are an heritage of the Lord: and the fruit of the womb is his reward.*) Generations of parents have relinquished their rights to train their children by leaving the teaching of values and skills to others. God tells us that we must do it!

We allowed Prayer to be removed from our schools that our tax dollars pay for, thus eliminating the reinforcement of Christ-like values taught at home and at church. We must prepare our children to read The Word Of God and to apply it to their daily lives. They should read The Word Of God before they enter school to enable them to compete successfully, thus succeeding in all areas of their lives.

This ministry is designed to foster good working and interpersonal relationships between God and our families - individually and collectively, parent and child with positive bonding, good communications skills, and excellent reading skills.

Your child will be grateful that the most important person to him on this earth took the time to teach him to read and gave him good principles based on The Word Of God. He will not have fear of the reading process, but will welcome opportunities to learn new things. He will have already been successful with his parents and will understand the importance of correction.

Parents, when you are diligent in administering these anointed materials, you can have a child skilled in reading and an obedient and teachable child. The benefits are endless!

You can also begin teaching your toddlers as early as 2 ½ years old or as soon as they begin to imitate reading, e.g. pretending to read, making up stories, turning pages, etc. The 90-Day schedule does not necessarily apply to teaching your toddlers, although we know miracles do happen!

READING WITH JESUS™
PREPARING TO
TEACH YOUR CHILD

PREPARING TO TEACH YOUR CHILD

PARENT TEACHING SESSION SCHEDULE
(PARENT(S) AND CHILD AT HOME)

1. Locate a place in the home where you will study on a regular basis. Decide on a time when you will work together each day.

2. Your child can sit on your lap with a book placed on his lap. You can sit together side-by-side with the book resting on your lap and on your child's lap.

   You can make this special place a classroom setting, especially if you have a chalkboard. You can write the letters and/or words on a chalkboard and your child can repeat the letter sounds and/or words after you, at the board, or read independently.

   You can vary the way you will teach within the special place in the home.

3. Inform the household and friends that this is your special time together and there should be no interruptions.

4. Warm-Up/Motivation

BE EXCITED ABOUT THIS SPECIAL TIME!

Make it a practice to pray together <u>before</u> you start to work with your child. (Take turns praying so that your child will get practice in praying with you and for you, himself and others.)

Before you start the teaching session tell your child what to expect, what you expect of him, and that you are going to evaluate the session together.

Discuss the rules of behavior <u>before</u> you start the sessions. In my workshops, the children are told what the rules are <u>before</u> they make a mistake in behavior. The rules of our READING WITH JESUS_{TM} *You Can Teach Your 4 or 5 Year Old Child To Read In 90 Days* © workshops are: 1) Listen 2) Watch and 3) Cooperate.

Set up clear rules also in your home, in addition to those mentioned above and/or extend the rules to your household to avoid unpleasantness and unnecessary distractions when we, as parents, do not set up rules for our child in advance. Review them often. Have your child repeat and memorize the rules. Parents, make sure you obey the rules as well. Remember, you are the example!

5. Go over the Introduction Activities regarding The Word Of God. Teach your child The Word!

6. The use of an audio or video tape recorder is an excellent way to evaluate your reading session. You will know how you sound and look while teaching your child. You will know whether or not you are being firm and gentle, while exercising patience, etc.

   You will have a record of how your child looks now and his voice to share with him when he is older.

7. Read the scripture(s) for each unit and encourage your child to memorize them along with you.

8. Most importantly parents, realize your child is learning to read for the first time. Use empathy - Put yourself in your child's shoes and remember when you were his/her age.

   It is a Tender Thing To Teach And Train A Child. Parents, I ask that you please exercise The Fruit Of The Spirit. Let's turn to Galatians 5:22 *But the fruit of the Spirit is love, joy, peace, longsuffering, gentleness, goodness, faith, 23. Meekness, temperance: against such there is no law.*

   Longsuffering is another word for Patience! There is a scripture that states, *But let patience have her perfect work, … (James 1:4)*

9. Ask The Lord to show you a balance on how to teach and train your child to avoid breaking your child's spirit. The Lord loves a just weight (balance). We must learn to be gentle and firm while teaching and training our children.

10. Now, let's start working!

   Work at least 15 minutes per day. When you start working with your child, you may have difficulty holding his attention. You may only be able to work for 5 minutes the first day. Do not become discouraged. Keep working until you build up to 15 minutes per day. **THE MORE YOUR CHILD EXPERIENCES SUCCESS, THE LONGER HE WILL WANT TO WORK.**

   This process increases the attention span of your child so that he will be able to receive the maximum amount of information from you, your pastor, and teachers at church and at school. My mother made a comment, "Just think, if a parent works with his child on any skill for at least 15 minutes per day, 5 days per week - the benefits are endless! Comradeship, love, and trust will be generated and shared as well as mastery of the skills taught."

READING WITH JESUS
TEACHING THE ALPHABET

TEACHING THE ALPHABET

WHAT IS THE ALPHABET?

Webster's New World Dictionary defines the alphabet as the letters of a language arranged in a traditional order.

How to teach the alphabet:

Remember, show excitement about this special time.

Be firm and gentle. Be patient. **Put yourself in your child's shoes.** Remember, your child may be learning the alphabet for the very first time. Try to remember how it feels when <u>you</u> are learning a new skill on your job, at home, etc.

1. Point to one letter at a time as the audio compact disk is playing, and have your child sing along with you and the compact disk. There are two parts of the Alphabet Song - Part I is a sing-along and Part II is a lullaby for bedtime and rest time, or whenever you wish.

2. Later, you say the letter out loud for extra practice. Tell your child to repeat each letter after you.

3. Each time your child repeats the letter or letters, you can use words of praise to compliment him, e.g., Praise The Lord! Excellent! Very Good! Great!, etc. This helps build self-confidence that he can do an excellent job, with God's help.

4. After some practice of your child repeating after you, ask him to tell you or show you the letters of the alphabet you have been working on or sing the alphabet song on his own.

5. Continue to practice the alphabet until your child can recognize the letters independently.

6. Whenever your child is incorrect in identifying a letter or letters of the alphabet, let him know it. Correct him. Tell him what they should be. Have him repeat the letter or letters after you. Compliment him. Then thank him for obeying you.

   This process shows your appreciation for your child responding to what you have asked him to do. It also helps develop in your child, a teachable spirit.

Your child must learn now that when he is in error, he should be shown the correct way to respond. This gives him a respect for correction.

7. Your child will have many opportunities to practice printing the letters of the alphabet while learning to read letter sounds, phonetic words, and sight words throughout the program, with Jesus!

    You may proceed with this burden-removing, yoke-destroying Power Of God Ministry tool. Hallelujah!

*   It is not necessary that your child learn the entire alphabet before you start teaching with these materials. However, play The Alphabet Song at least twice per day. This will also help your child learn the alphabet.

READING WITH JESUS
Unit Introduction Activities

UNIT INTRODUCTION ACTIVITIES

Unit One

PARENTS: The Bible states, *Train up a child in the way he should go: and when he is old he will not depart from it. (Proverbs 22:6)*

1. Parents, explain to <u>your</u> child that he will be learning to read and that you will be teaching him. He will start off with the scripture(s) for each unit; then learn letter sounds that will help him read words by sounding them out (phonetic words), then learn to read sight words (words your child must learn to read by sight), and finally whole sentences. Let him know that he will be able to read scriptures from The Holy Bible, sentences in other books and magazines, signs on billboards and shopping centers, etc.

   Always build up <u>your</u> child's confidence and tell your child, on a regular basis, that he can learn to read.

2. Stress to your child the scripture, Philippians 4:13, I can do all things through Christ which strengtheneth me.

   Have your child repeat the scripture out loud. Tell your child that he can do all things through Christ which strengtheneth him. (The Greek definition for **Christ is The Anointed One and His Anointings.**)

   Tell your child that he can do anything if he tries. (Be sure to tell him that we are talking about good things, not bad things.) Ask your child to tell you some things he would like to learn to do. Ask your child to draw a picture of the things he would like to learn to do. He is learning goal setting skills. You may not understand the picture he draws, but ask him to tell you what he has drawn. Make a big deal out of the drawing! Be excited!

   Ask your child if he believes he can do all things through Christ which strengtheneth him.

   You are developing in your child good oral expression and good communications skills. You want your child to always feel free to communicate with you.

You will learn how your child feels about various subjects. This will make it easier for you to train him. Your child will learn how you feel about various subjects, thus, you will be his role model. (You are your child's role model, whether the model is good or not.) You are to set the positive example for your child.

Philippians 4:13
I can do all things through Christ
which strengtheneth me.

UNIT TWO

***PARENTS:* KEEP UP THE GOOD WORK!!** *Isaiah 54:13 And thy children shall be taught of the Lord; and great shall be the peace of thy children.*

Discuss the sight words with your child.

You can look the words up in the dictionary, while your child is with you. This will prepare him for good dictionary and research skills. Read the definitions to him. (If there are any letter sounds or words he has learned thus far, have him point to them and read the sounds of the letters and/or read the words.)

Parents, ask your child the following questions:

1. What is love?
   Parents, tell your child that you love her/him.
   Parents, ask your child to tell you he loves you.
   Thank your child after he tells you that he loves you.

   (Parents, you cannot believe the number of parents and children who cannot express Godly love toward each other. Some parents have never experienced a true Godly love of a father and mother.)

2. Ask your child what love feels like to him/her.

   Parents, hug your child.
   Parents, ask your child to hug you. Thank your child after he hugs you. Parents kiss your child. Ask your child to give you a kiss. Thank your child after he kisses you.

   You must teach your child that God loves him/her and that he/she is to love The Lord. It is also important that your child knows that you love him. If he believes that you love him, he will love himself.
   1 John 4:7 ... for love is of God.

   Mark 12:30,31 And thou shalt love the Lord thy God with all thy heart, and with all thy soul, and with all thy mind, and with all thy strength: this is the first commandment. 31.

And the second is like, namely this, *Thou shalt love thy neighbor as thyself.* There is none other commandment greater than these.

Our children will not grow up abusing their children or their spouses. They will also learn how to speak pleasantly to people; edifying one another. *1 Corinthians 8:1 ... Love edifies.* They will learn the value of love and the value of the human being. They will treat others as they would like to be treated.

3. Ask your child what the word 'obey' means.

4. How does it feel when you obey Daddy, Mommy, Grandfather or Grandmother, Aunt, Uncle, your Pastor, etc.?

5. Parents, tell your child how it feels when you do the right things.

   When your child knows that you try to do the right things, he will do the same. If you respect authority, your child can also respect authority.

   Parents, when your child knows that you receive instruction and correction from your pastors, employers and others in authority, he will do the same. (*Proverbs 22:6 Train up a child in the way he should go: and when he is old, he will not depart from it.*)

6. Tell your child how important it is to obey The Word of God. (*Proverbs 3:7-8 Be not wise in thine own eyes: fear the Lord, and depart from evil. 8. It shall be health to thy navel, and marrow to thy bones.*)

7. Explain to your child that parents have to obey as well. The responsibility of parents in the scripture is critical. *Colossians 3:20* is extremely important! When The Holy Bible tells our children to obey their parents in all things, do make sure that you are teaching and modeling good habits and behavior. **Make sure you are giving them Godly instruction.** *Psalm 127:3 states, Lo, children are an heritage of the Lord; and the fruit of the womb is His reward.* He has given them to us to train correctly.

8. Does it make Daddy and Mommy feel happy or sad when you obey them?

9. Have your child make a confession that he will obey Daddy and Mommy. Have your child point to the word "obey" in the Unit Two Sight Words Section.

   Have your child point to the word "Daddy" in the Unit Two Sight Words Section.

   Have your child point to the word "Mommy" in the Unit Two Sight Words Section.

1 John 4:7
...for love is of God.

Colossians 3:20
Children, obey your parents in all things: for this is well pleasing unto the Lord.

Ephesians 6:1
Children, obey your parents in the Lord: for this is right.

UNIT THREE

PARENTS: Isn't this fun?!!! *(Psalm 127:3 Lo, children are an heritage of the Lord: and the fruit of the womb is His reward.)*

Discuss the sight words with your child.

You can look the words up in the dictionary, while your child is with you. This will prepare him for good dictionary and research skills. Read the definitions to him. (If there are any letter sounds or words he has learned thus far, have him point to them and read the sounds of the letters and/or read the words.)

Parents, in addition to loving your children, you must also believe in them and believe The Lord will make sure that they will succeed. *(Galatians 5:6 ... but faith which worketh by love.)*

Our children want us to believe in them. We are created in God's image. *Genesis 1:27 states, God created man in His own image, in the image of God created He him; male and female created He them. Hebrews 11:6 But without faith it is impossible to please Him: for he that cometh to God must believe that He is, and that He is a rewarder of them that diligently seek Him.* The Lord desires that we have faith in Him and our children desire us to have faith in them. (We are made in His image.) When we let our children know that we have faith in them, they can and will excel. It also increases their love for us. Again, Galatians 5:6b states, ... *but faith which worketh by love.* Loving our children and having faith in our children will enable them to produce many good things and they will succeed in life, "With The Word Of God".

Continue to tell your child he can do all things through Christ (The Anointed One and His Anointings) which strengtheneth him. The more he hears you say that he can do it and you believe he can do all things, he will accomplish more. *Romans 10:17 So then faith cometh by hearing and hearing by the Word of God.*

Mark 11:22 ... Have faith in God.

Unit Four

CONGRATULATIONS PARENTS FOR YOUR LOVE, TIME AND LABOR IN TRAINING YOUR CHILD FOR EXCELLENCE AND SUCCESS IN LIFE, TEACHING HIM/HER TO READ WITH THE WORD OF GOD!!!

Jeremiah 32:39-40 And God will give them one heart, and one way, that they may fear me forever, for the good of them, and of their children after them. 40. And I will make an everlasting covenant with them, that I will not turn away from them, to do them good; … .

Discuss the sight words with your child.

You can look the words up in the dictionary, while your child is with you. This will prepare him for good dictionary and research skills. Read the definitions to him. (If there are any letter sounds or words he has learned thus far, have him point to them and read the sounds of the letters and/or read the words.)

It is a blessing to teach your child to read while using The Holy Bible. The principles that he/she are learning will equip him/her to be alert and aware of evil. They will not be deceived by the many voices in the world. They will know certain Holy Bible principles that can keep him/her out of trouble. He/she will know Jesus' voice. The Bible states in *John 10:3-5 To Him the porter openeth; and the sheep hear his voice; and he calleth his own sheep by name, and leadeth them out. 4. And when he putteth forth his own sheep, he goeth before them, and the sheep follow; for they know his voice. 5. And a stranger will they not follow, but will flee from him; for they know not the voice of strangers.*

Another principle in the Holy Bible is that Jesus Christ is Lord *(Philippians 2:11)*. *John 1:1 In the beginning was the Word, and the Word was with God, and the Word was God.* . This scripture can be read, In the beginning was Jesus, and Jesus was with God and Jesus was God.

John 1:14 states, And the Word was made flesh, and dwelt among us, and we beheld His glory, the glory as of the only begotten of the Father, full of grace and truth. John 1:14 tells us that The Word is Jesus made flesh.

Continue to teach, encourage and train your child!

Psalm 33:2 Praise The Lord …
John 21:7 … It is The Lord…
Psalm 100:3 … The Lord He is God: …
Philippians 2:11 … Jesus Christ is Lord,

Unit Five

PARENTS, KEEP UP THE GOOD WORK! THIS IS THE LAST INSTRUCTIONAL UNIT IN THIS DEVELOPMENTAL SERIES. YOU ARE SUCH A BLESSING TO YOUR CHILD! YOU HAVE BEEN TEACHING YOUR CHILD TO READ, WHILE TRAINING HIM/HER TO FOLLOW THE PRINCIPLES FROM THE WORD OF GOD!

Hebrews 4:12 For the Word Of God is quick and powerful, and sharper than any two-edged sword … .)

The inclusion of The Holy Bible in these parent-administered developmental reading materials, has sped up the learning process. As your child has been taught by you, he/she has learned quickly and completely.

Parents, the most effective tool (and one of the "Fruit of The Spirit") in teaching your child to read and in training your child in the way he should go is, **joy**! The Webster's Dictionary describes **joy** as a very glad feeling; happiness; great pleasure; delight; rejoice; enjoy; be full of joy; make joyful.

Joy gives us strength. ***Nehemiah 8:10 … for joy of the Lord is your strength.***

The Webster's Dictionary describes **strength** as the state or quality of being strong; force; power; vigor; the power to resist strain, stress, etc.; toughness and durability; the power to resist attack.

Joy energizes. It makes you want to go further. Joy actually gives you the strength to complete tasks, love, obey, exercise your faith, etc. Always rejoice when your child responds correctly while learning to read or when he completes a task at home. This encourages him.

God speaks things into being and so must we. He spoke things into existence in the entire First Chapter of Genesis. For example, verse *3. And God said, Let there be light: and there was light. (After the light came to be,) 4. And God saw the light, that it was good: and God divided the light from the darkness. 5. And He called the light Day, and the darkness He called Night. And the evening and the morning were the first day.*

This scripture let's us know that we should speak good things into existence for our children. For example, we must confess that our children will grow in the Lord, learn to read, succeed in school and in church and they will grow in the nurture and the admonition of The Lord. (*Ephesians 6:4 And, ye fathers, provoke not your children to wrath: but bring them up in the nurture and admonition of the Lord.*) Before this comes to pass, we are confessing positive words over our children and exercising our faith. Thus, when this comes to pass, we can find ways to bless and reward our children and Praise The Lord!

Proverbs 18:21 tells us that, *Death and life are in the power of the tongue: and they that love it shall eat the fruit thereof.*

We can either speak life words over our children or death words over them. The Holy Bible tells us that Jesus came that we might have abundant life, *John 10:10 … I am come that they might have life, and that they might have it more abundantly.*

We must choose life-filled words to build up our children that will make them increase in the knowledge of The Lord. This will ensure <u>God-esteem</u> and <u>good success</u>!

What are we saying to our children?

Nehemiah 8:10 ... for the joy of the Lord is your strength.
Genesis 1:3-29 ... And God said, ...
Matthew 25:23 ... the joy of your Lord.

READING WITH JESUS
Sound Key

SOUND KEY

(In Order of Presentation)

UNIT	CONSONANTS
ONE * Vowel: **a** in Adam	**m** in miracles **n** in neighbor **c** in Christ **p** in peace
TWO * Vowel: **u** in understanding	**h** in heaven **r** in righteousness **f** in faith **g** in God
THREE * Vowel **i** in Israel	**t** in temple **s** in Savior **k** in Kingdom **w** in Word Of God
FOUR * Vowel **o** in obtain	**b** in babe **x** in ox **d** in David **q** in queen
FIVE * Vowel **e** in Esther	**v** in victory **j** in Jesus **y** in year **z** in Zion **l** in love

READING WITH JESUS
Reading Phonetic Words

READING PHONETIC WORDS

WHAT IS A PHONETIC WORD?

A phonetic word is a word a person must be able to read by sounding out the letters in a word.

How to teach letter sounds:

Remember, show excitement about this special time!.

Be firm and gentle. **Increase your patience level!**

1. Point to one letter at a time.

2. Say the letter sound out loud.

3. Tell your child to repeat each letter after you.

4. Each time your child repeats the letter sound correctly after you, compliment him/her. You can use praise words, e.g., Praise The Lord! Excellent! Very Good! Great!, etc. (This helps build God-esteem.)

    (Rearrange the order of the letters so you will not think your child has mastered the skills and he has only memorized the order of the words on the page.)

    (When my daughter, Leigh Ann, my precious gift from heaven, was assisting me with a group of pre-school aged children, I overheard her complimenting the children when they repeated the sounds correctly. When she was teaching the letter sound of short **a**, and the children would either repeat the letter sound correctly after her, or could make the letter sound correctly themselves, she would compliment them by using words that begin with the same letter. For example, short **a**, Leigh Ann would compliment them by saying, "**A**bsolutely Marvelous!" In the case of the letter **f**, she would compliment by saying, "**F**antastic!")

    This is an excellent way to reinforce the letter sounds! I am sure The Lord will show you other excellent ways to reinforce the letter sounds as you continue to compliment your child.

    Vary the order of the letter sounds.

6. After some practice of the child repeating after you, then ask him to make the sounds of the letters on his own.

7. Continue to practice the letter sounds until your child can read the sounds independently.

Whenever your child makes a letter sound incorrectly, let him know it. Correct him. Tell him what it should be. Have him repeat the letter sound correctly after you. Compliment him. Then, thank him for obeying you.

This process helps develop in your child, a teachable spirit. The child must learn now that when he is in error he should be corrected.

Reinforcement Activities:

I. Make a letter card for each letter sound your child is learning. (3x5, 5x8, etc.)

  A. Use brightly colored markers.

  B. Place them in your child's bedroom in a place where he will see them before he goes to sleep and when he awakes.

  C. Have your child read the letter cards at night before he prays and in the morning after he greets The Lord.

  Make another set of cards and store them in a card file box so your child can study them on his/her own.

II. Make sure to teach your child about taking good care of his letter cards and his books.

  A. Have your child locate the letters he knows in the Holy Bible, newspapers, magazines, etc.

  B. Have your child count the number of the same letters he locates in the Holy Bible, newspapers, magazines, etc. (For example: *John 14:6 ... I a*m *the way, the truth, and the life: no* m*an co*m*eth unto the Father, but by* m*e.*)

  (Ask your child how many times he sees the letter sound m in this scripture? Help him/her count the number of sounds. -- Answer: The number of m sounds in this scripture is 4.)

Discuss John 14:6 with your child.

C. Have your child use safe highlighters to mark the letters he can sound out.

D. Have your child draw a circle around the letter sounds he can read independently and/or draw a line under the letter sounds he can read independently. (Select the books you wish him to use.) (Explain to your child that he is not to select and/or write in a book without permission or write on the walls.)

E. Have your child write the letters he can recognize and pronounce correctly independent of you. (If your child can produce a letter sound correctly and independently, he can write it.) Most children will have the desire to write if they are exposed to writing.

Show your child how to write the letters on a sheet of paper;
Have your child trace the letters or print the words free-style.

Print the words on a chalkboard and have your child trace the words or print the words free-style. Your child can make letter cards using 3x5 or 5x8 cards and bright markers.

(Note: When your child begins to write the letter, it helps him retain it. My daughter, Leigh Ann, who assists me in workshops says, "When a child writes the letters, they get stuck in his brain.")

When your child writes a letter, it releases energy to help him remember the word.

The goal is not only for your child to become skilled in reading words and sentences with comprehension, but to write words and sentences and to eventually write stories, take notes, take dictation, become proficient in spelling, etc.

Habakkuk 2:2-3 ... Write the vision, and make it plain upon tables, that he may run that readeth it. 3. For the vision is yet for an appointed time, but at the end it shall speak, and not lie: though it tarry, wait for it; because it will surely come, it will not tarry.

F. Dictate the letter sounds to your child.

G. Have your child think of words that begin with the letter sounds he is learning. (For example, m in miracle, Messiah, Moses, Mary, mayonnaise, money, etc.)

H. Have your child cut out pictures of words that start with the letter sounds you are teaching him.

I. Have your child paste pictures on construction paper. (Note: Select the magazines, books, etc., you want your child to use.)

Blending (Two-Letter Sounds)

BEFORE TEACHING YOUR CHILD TO BLEND LETTER SOUNDS, MAKE SURE HE/SHE CAN PRODUCE SINGLE SOUNDS CORRECTLY AND INDEPENDENTLY. IF HE EXPERIENCES DIFFICULTY, REVIEW THE SOUNDS HE DOES NOT KNOW.

DO NOT PROCEED TO THIS SECTION UNTIL YOUR CHILD CAN PRODUCE SINGLE-LETTER SOUNDS ON HIS OWN.

How to teach blending of two-letter sounds (one consonant and one vowel):

1. Point to the first letter in the set.

2. Produce the first sound.

   Attack the first letter sound (producing the letter sound, without hesitation). This is the first process in "word attack skills". *Matthew 11:12 ... the Kingdom of heaven suffereth violence, and the violent take it by force.* **Remember, the enemy does not want our children to read because the skill of reading will enable them to read The Word Of God and <u>find out who God really is</u> and <u>who they really are</u>!**

   Hold the sound while moving your finger until you reach the second sound.

   Continue to practice with your child until he can blend the two-letter sounds together independently.

3. Start off blending the two letters slowly, then as your child becomes more skilled, have him to blend the letters faster.

Reinforcement Activities:

I. Make a blending letter card after your child learns to blend two-letter sounds together, independently. (one consonant and one vowel/one vowel and one consonant) (3x5, 5x8, etc.)

For example: m   a
               a   m

   A. Use brightly colored markers.

   B. Place them in your child's bedroom in a place where he will see them before he goes to sleep and when he awakes.

C. Have your child read the letter cards at night before he prays and in the morning after he greets The Lord.

D. Make another set of cards and store them in a card file box so your child can study them on his/her own or place the cards on the refrigerator, doors, mirrors, etc.

II. Have your child write the letters he can blend independently.

(I always tell parents if their child can read letter sounds (blends) correctly, he can write them.) Most children will have the desire to write when they are exposed to writing letters, blends, and words.

A. Show your child how to write the letters he can blend on a sheet of paper.

B. Have your child trace the letters he can blend or print them free-style.

Write the letters your child can blend on a chalkboard and have your child trace the letters or print them free-style on the chalkboard or paper.

(Remember: When your child writes the letters he can blend, they get stuck in his brain.)

BLENDING (Three-Letter Sounds)

DO NOT PROCEED TO THIS SECTION UNTIL YOUR CHILD CAN BLEND TWO-LETTER SOUNDS INDEPENDENTLY.

How to teach blending of three-letter sounds: (two consonants and one vowel)

While teaching your child to read three-letter words, e.g., cap, cat, box, fox, etc., you and your child can have a <u>picture hunt</u> using the newspaper, magazines, etc. Make a <u>picture chest</u> or file that contains pictures of the words your child is learning to read. (This activity can also be used while learning to read the single phonetic letters by locating pictures that begin with the beginning sound, e.g., locate a picture in the magazine that begins with the letter <u>m</u>.) Ask your child to find a box on a page in a magazine. You can also have your child draw pictures of the above words.

1. Point to the first two letters in the set.

2. Blend the first two letters. Attack the first two letter sounds, without hesitation.

Hold the two blended sounds while moving your finger across the line until you reach the third sound; then slowly blend in the third sound.

For example: ca   n

ma   n

3. Continue to practice with your child until he can smoothly blend the first two letter sounds with the third letter sound.

4. Start off blending the three sounds together slowly, then as your child becomes more skilled, have him blend the letters faster.

Reinforcement Activities:

I. <u>Picture Chest Activities</u>. You can print a word on a piece of paper. Do not tell your child the word, but tell him to either draw a picture of the word or locate a picture of the word in the picture chest.

II. Make a blending letter card (3x5, 5x8, etc.) for each three sounds your child is learning to read.

For example: ca   n
              ma   n

A. Use brightly colored markers.

B. Place them in your child's bedroom in a place where he will see them before he goes to sleep and when he/she awakes.

C. Have your child blend the letter cards in the morning and at night.

D. Make another set of cards and store them in a card file box so your child can study them on his/her own.

E. Have your child write the three letters of the blends he can read independently. (This helps develop dictation skills and note taking.)

If your child can produce a letter sound correctly, he can write it. Most children have the desire to write when they are exposed to writing.

F. Use large paper and child-size crayon.

Show your child how to write the three letters (phonetic words) on a sheet of paper.

Have your child trace the letter blends (phonetic words) or print the words free-style. Write the letter blends (phonetic words) on a chalkboard and have your child trace the words or print them free-style.

(**Remember**: When your child begins to write the letters, it helps him retain them.)

When your child writes the letter blends (phonetic words), it releases energy to help him/her remember the letters and words.

Habakkuk 2:2-3. 2. ... Write the vision, and make it plain upon tables, that he may run that readeth it. 3. For the vision is yet for an appointed time, but at the end it shall speak, and not lie: though it tarry, Wait for it; because it will surely come, it will not tarry.

G. Your child can also make blending letter cards using 3x5, 5x8, etc., cards.

H. When your child can blend three-letter sounds together, have your child write the phonetic words the letters make.

For example: ca n (can)

  ma n (man)

I. Have your child make phonetic word cards.

J. Have your child practice reading the phonetic words quickly and smoothly.

Start off blending the three sounds together slowly, then as your child becomes more skilled, have him/her to read the phonetic words faster..

READING WITH JESUS
READING SIGHT WORDS

READING SIGHT WORDS

WHAT IS A SIGHT WORD?

A sight word is a word a person must be able to read when he sees it.

How to teach sight words:

1. Point to one word at a time.

2. Read the word out loud.

3. Tell your child to repeat each word.

4. Each time your child repeats the sight words correctly, after you, compliment him/her. You can use words of praise, e.g., Praise The Lord! Excellent! Very Good! Great!, etc. (This helps build God-esteem.)

5. Vary the order of the sight words.

6. After your child has had some practice repeating after you, ask him to read the words.

7. Continue to practice the words until your child can read them on his/her own.

8. Whenever your child reads a word incorrectly let him/her know it. Correct him/her. Tell him/her what it should be. Have him/her repeat the word correctly after you. Compliment him/her. Then thank him/her for trying again.

   This process helps develop in your child a teachable spirit. Your child must learn <u>now</u> that when he is in error he should be corrected.

Reinforcement Activities:

I. Make a word card for each word your child is learning. (3x5 or 5x8, etc.)

   A. Use brightly colored markers.

B. Place them in your child's bedroom in a location where he will see them before he goes to sleep and when he awakes. Have your child read the word cards in the morning and at night.

C. Make another set of cards and store them in a card file box so your child can study them on his/her own.

(Make sure to teach your child about taking good care of his/her word cards and his books.)

D. Have your child locate the words he knows in the Holy Bible, newspapers, magazines, on billboards, grocery and shopping mall signs, etc.

E. Have your child count the number of the same word he locates in the Holy Bible, newspapers, magazines, etc. (For example: *John 14:6 ... I am the way, the truth, and the life: no man cometh unto the Father, but by me.* (Ask your child, "How many times do you see the word the in this scripture?" Count the words with your child. The answer is 4 times.) Discuss the scripture.

F. Have your child use highlighters to mark the words in the Holy Bible and other books he can read; draw a circle around the words he can read; and/or draw a line under the words he can read.

G. Select the books you wish him to use. Explain to your child that he is not to select a book without your permission or write on the walls.

II. Have your child write the words he can read. (If your child can read a word, he can write it.) Once you expose him/her to writing, he/she will have the desire to write.

A. Show your child how to write the words on a piece of paper.

B. Have your child trace the words or print the words free-style.

C. Print the words on a chalkboard and have your child trace the words or print the words free-style.

D. Your child can also make word cards using 3x5 or 5x8 cards and use bright markers.

When your child writes a word, it releases energy to help him remember the word.

The goal is not only for your child to become skilled in reading words and sentences with comprehension, but to write words and sentences and to eventually write stories, take notes, take dictation, become proficient in spelling, etc.

Habakkuk 2:2-3 states, 2. ... Write the vision, and make it plain upon tables, that he may run that readeth it. 3. For the vision is yet for an appointed time, but at the end it shall speak, and not lie: though it tarry, wait for it; because it will surely come, it will not tarry.

E. Have your child learn to spell the words.

F. Dictate the words to your child.

G. Dictate sentences to your child when he has learned enough phonetic and sight words.

H. Have your child develop sentences on his own.

READING WITH JESUS
Reading Sentences

READING SENTENCES

WHAT IS A SENTENCE?

A sentence is a group of words that make a complete thought.

How to teach your child to read sentences:

1. Point to each word and have your child read each word in the sentence. Vary the order of the sentences. (Continue this several times.)

2. Have your child point to each word and read them. Vary the order. (Continue this several times.)

3. Have your child read the sentences without pointing to the words. Vary the order. (Continue this several times.)

4. Explain to your child that he should begin to read the sentences smoothly, just as he speaks, and not one word at a time, choppy or slow. Encourage him to read smoothly and with expression.

5. Stress good posture and the proper way to hold the book while reading. Have your child stand while reading.

6. Now that your child is reading, it is important that he understands what he reads. Ask your child questions to make sure he understands what he is reading. For example:

Pam can nap.

Pam can do all things through Christ which strengtheneth her.

I can.

The kinds of reading comprehension questions you can ask are as follows:

Who can nap?

Ans.   Pam can nap.

Who can?

Ans.   I can.

Can Pam do all things?

Ans.   Yes, Pam can do all things.

Why do you think Pam can do all things?
(This is an inference type question. It requires some thought. This type of question does not have a yes or no answer.)

Ans.   Pam can do all things because Christ strengthens her to do all things.

Have your child point to the sentences that answer the questions.

Reinforcement Activities:

I.   Use word cards (phonetic and sight).

II. Have your child develop sentences from the word cards.

III. Have your child write the words and/or sentences he makes out of his word cards.

IV. Have your child read out loud the sentences he makes out of his word cards.

V.   Have your child locate the scriptures in The Holy Bible for a specific lesson.

   A. For example: ***Philippians 4:13 I can do all things through Christ which strengtheneth me.***

   Have your child highlight the scripture.

   Have your child spell the words out loud. (Have an oral spelling quiz.)

B. Dictate words and sentences to your child.

C. Have your child take notes in church services.

(Your child may not spell all the words correctly, at first, but that is alright.) Just be sure and correct the words he spells incorrectly. Before you correct your child, tell him he did an excellent job! Then gently show him the correct way to spell the words. Add the new words to the card file, look them up in the dictionary for definitions, and continue to teach your child new words he encounters.)

(During the time I was teaching my daughter, my precious gift from heaven, Leigh Ann, to read at an early age "With The Word Of God", she amazed me at an evening service. She looked up at me and asked, John what? I looked at her, then looked down at her paper and she was actually taking notes, including the scriptural references of the teaching from the pastor. Leigh Ann had observed me, her grandmother and other members of our local assembly taking notes and studying "The Word Of God". She was imitating and performing what she observed. What an excellent compliment when The Lord allows you to see the fruit of your labor! Praise Ye The Lord!)

The goal is not only for your child to become skilled in reading words and sentences with comprehension, but to write words and sentences and to eventually write stories, take notes, take dictation, become proficient in spelling, etc.

Habakkuk 2:2-3 states, 2. ... Write the vision, and make it plain upon tables, that he may run that readeth it. 3. For the vision is yet for an appointed time, but at the end it shall speak, and not lie: though it tarry, wait for it; because it will surely come, it will not tarry.

READING WITH JESUS
APPENDIX

INSTRUCTIONS FOR THE SUPPLEMENTARY WORD LIST

APPENDIX

Instructions for The Supplementary Word List

Parents, the Child's Book contains an additional listing of most frequently used words which your child needs to be able to read and/or will be tested on these words. He/she must be able to read them, without hesitation. If your child hesitates while he is being tested, he could be marked incorrect even if he does know the word. Teach him to read quickly and correctly. Give your child experience in completing a task within a specific period of time. This exercise will help make him a competitive student and he will not be afraid of the testing process.

Parents, teach your child the words on the Supplementary Word List as you have taught him previously from the Parents' Book. This time you can locate scriptures in The Holy Bible that contain the words you are going to teach and develop your own lesson plans. Locate scriptures so that your child can continue to read from The Word Of God!

Up to this point, your child has had a great deal of practice with phonetic sounds, words and sight words. By this time, he should be more than able to sound out phonetic words he may encounter. *Continue to review the phonetic sounds of letters and blending the sounds together to make words and he can become an independent reader if he has not become one already.*

(Remember Philippians 4:13. I can do all things through Christ which strengtheneth me.)

We do not know when the miracle of independent advanced reading will take place, but look for it to happen soon!

Remember, your child must be able to read phonetic words without hesitation. Remind your child to attack the first letter sound or sounds in order to read the words quickly. Also remember if your child hesitates during testing, he could be marked incorrect even though he knows the word.

Have your child practice reading at a fast pace to ensure that he will be competitive when he is faced with testing of letters, letter sounds and words (phonetic and sight words). This type of practice will determine where your child will be placed in reading.

Continue To Be Blessed By The Word Of God!

This work was inspired by The Holy Spirit and influenced by Metra-Summerhays Publishing Company.

PARENTS' CERTIFICATE

Parents' Certificate

_____

Name(s) of Parent(s)

You have successfully taught your child to read with the developmental version of
READING WITH JESUS™ ***You Can Teach Your 4 or 5 Year Old***
Child To Read In 90 Days ©!

Proverbs 24:3

Through wisdom is an house builded; and by understanding it is established. 4. And by knowledge shall the chambers be filled with all precious and pleasant riches.

God Bless You and Congratulations!!!

_____

Date

Rev. Dr. Carol McIlwain Edwards
Rhema Reading Services LLC